ChordTime® Piano

Disney

LEVEL 2B

Arranged by Nancy and Randall Faber

This book belongs to: _____

Production Coordinator: Jon Ophoff
Editor: Isabel Otero Bowen
Design and Illustration: Terpstra Design, San Francisco
Engraving: Dovetree Productions, Inc.

A NOTE TO TEACHERS

ChordTime® Piano Disney brings together contemporary and classic Disney hits arranged for the Level 2B pianist. In the words of Walt Disney, "There is more treasure in books than in all the pirates' loot on Treasure Island." This book offers musical treasure for piano students with blockbusters from *Beauty and the Beast, Moana, The Lion King, Tangled, The Little Mermaid,* and more.

Students develop confidence at the piano through mastery of scales and chords. The *ChordTime Piano* series explores these fundamentals in a setting of inspiring songs. Correlating to Level 2B of the Piano Adventures® method, the pieces are in the keys of C, G, and F major and feature I, IV, and V⁷ chords with various accompaniment patterns. Each section of the book introduces a major key with scale and chord warm-ups for the pieces that follow.

ChordTime® Piano is part of the PreTime to BigTime Supplementary Piano Library arranged by Faber & Faber. The series allows students to enjoy a favorite style at their current level of study. ChordTime books are available in the following styles: *Popular, Classics, Favorites, Rock 'n Roll, Jazz & Blues, Ragtime & Marches, Hymns, Kids' Songs, Christmas, Jewish Favorites,* and the *Faber Studio Collection.*

Visit us at **PianoAdventures.com**.

Helpful Hints:

1. The chord warm-ups for a given key should be played daily before practicing the songs.

2. The student can be asked to identify the I, IV, and V7 chords in each song and write the correct chord symbol below the bass staff.

3. The student can be encouraged to identify any other chord that he or she is able to recognize and to label it accordingly (e.g., the occasional root position major or minor chord). It is helpful to encourage an atmosphere of discovery.

THE PRETIME TO BIGTIME PIANO LIBRARY

PreTime® Piano	= Primer Level
PlayTime® Piano	= Level 1
ShowTime® Piano	= Level 2A
ChordTime® Piano	= Level 2B
FunTime® Piano	= Level 3A–3B
BigTime® Piano	= Level 4 & above

ISBN 978-1-61677-700-5

Printed in U.S.A.

TABLE OF CONTENTS

I, IV, V⁷ Chords in the Key of C

Supercalifragilisticexpialidocious (from *Mary Poppins*) 4

Belle (from *Beauty and the Beast*) 6

Be Our Guest (from *Beauty and the Beast*)...............8

I've Got a Dream (from *Tangled*) 10

I, IV, V⁷ Chords in the Key of G

I Just Can't Wait to Be King (from *The Lion King*) 13

Bella Notte (from *Lady and the Tramp*) 16

Circle of Life (from *The Lion King*) 18

I, IV, V⁷ Chords in the Key of F

The Bare Necessities (from *The Jungle Book*)..........................21

Fathoms Below (from *The Little Mermaid*) 24

How Far I'll Go (from *Moana*) 26

Music Dictionary 29

Key of C

C Scale Warm-up: Play **H.A.** (Hands Alone), then **H.T.** (Hands Together).

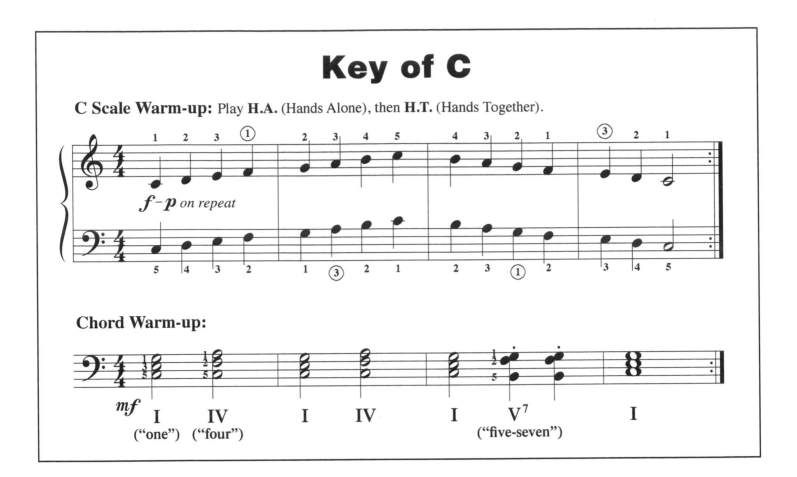

f - p on repeat

Chord Warm-up:

mf I IV I IV I V⁷ I

("one") ("four") ("five-seven")

Supercalifragilisticexpialidocious

from *MARY POPPINS*

WHO SAID THIS?
You know, you can say it backwards,
which is Dociousaliexpiisticfragicalirupes —
but that's going a bit too far, don't you think?

Words and Music by
RICHARD M. SHERMAN
and ROBERT B. SHERMAN

Lively

p *mf*

mp Su - per - cal - i - frag - il - is - tic - ex - pi - al - i - do - cious!

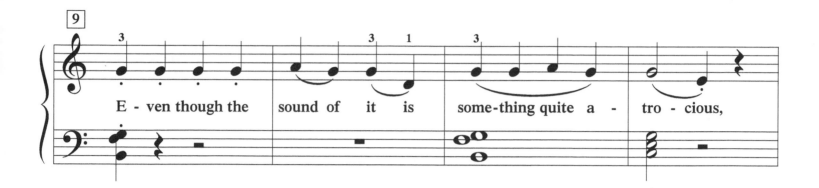

E - ven though the sound of it is some-thing quite a - tro - cious,

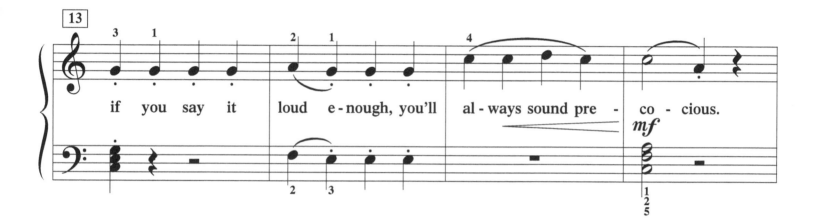

if you say it loud e - nough, you'll al - ways sound pre - co - cious. *mf*

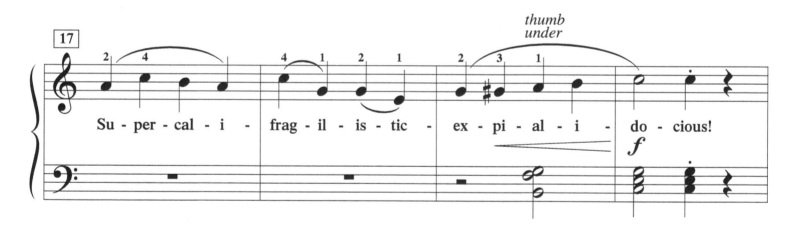

thumb under

Su - per - cal - i - frag - il - is - tic - ex - pi - al - i - do - cious! *f*

p *ritardando* *a tempo* *f* *8va- - - - - - - - - - - - - - - -*

6

Belle

from *Beauty and the Beast*

Music by ALAN MENKEN
Lyrics by HOWARD ASHMAN

WHO SAID THIS?
This is the day your
dreams come true.

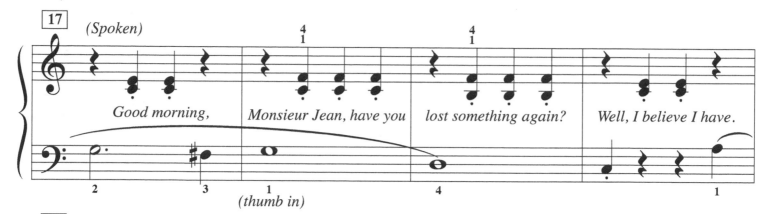

17 *(Spoken)*

Good morning, Monsieur Jean, have you lost something again? Well, I believe I have.

(thumb in)

21

The problem is, I can't remember what. Oh well, I'm sure it'll come

25

to me. Where are you off to? To return this book

29

ritardando   D.C. al Coda

to Père Robert. It's about two lovers in fair Verona. Sounds boring!

mf   *f*

Coda

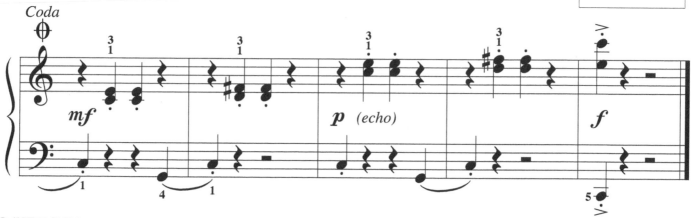

mf   *p (echo)*   *f*

ANSWER: Gaston

FF3042

Be Our Guest

from *Beauty and the Beast*

WHO SAID THIS?
And now, we invite you to relax.
Let us pull up a chair, as the dining
room proudly presents…your dinner.

Music by ALAN MENKEN
Words by HOWARD ASHMAN

Cheerfully

f Be our guest! Be our guest! Put our

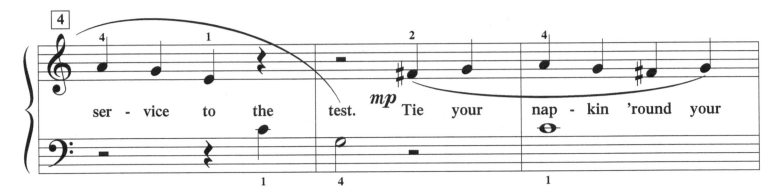

ser - vice to the test. *mp* Tie your nap - kin 'round your

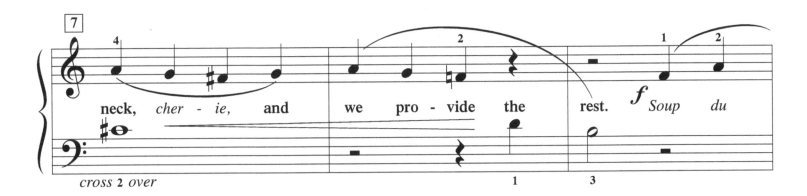

neck, *cher - ie,* and we pro - vide the rest. *f* *Soup du*

cross **2** over

jour! *Hot hors d'oeuvres!* Why, we on - ly live to serve. Try the *mp*

FF3042

grey stuff. It's de - li - cious! Don't be - lieve me? Ask the

cross 2 over

dish - es! They can sing! They can dance! Af - ter all, Miss, this is

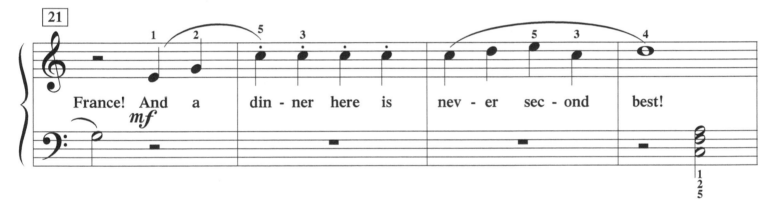

France! And a din - ner here is nev - er sec - ond best!

cross over

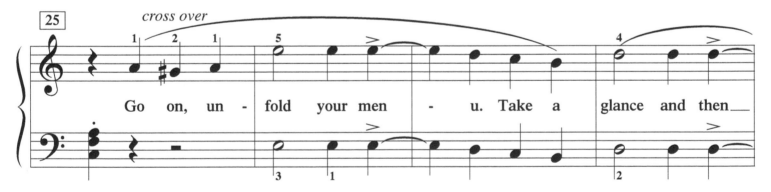

Go on, un - fold your men - u. Take a glance and then

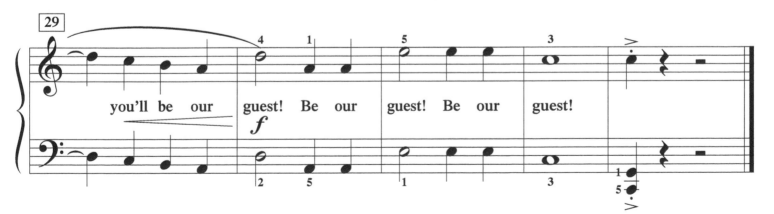

you'll be our guest! Be our guest! Be our guest!

I've Got a Dream

from *Tangled*

Music by ALAN MENKEN
Lyrics by GLENN SLATER

WHO SAID THIS?
Something brought you here,
Flynn Rider. Call it what you
will—fate, destiny…

Slowly and freely

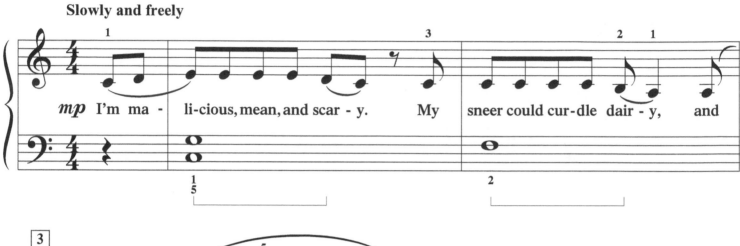

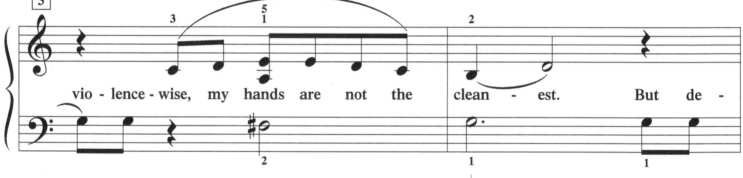

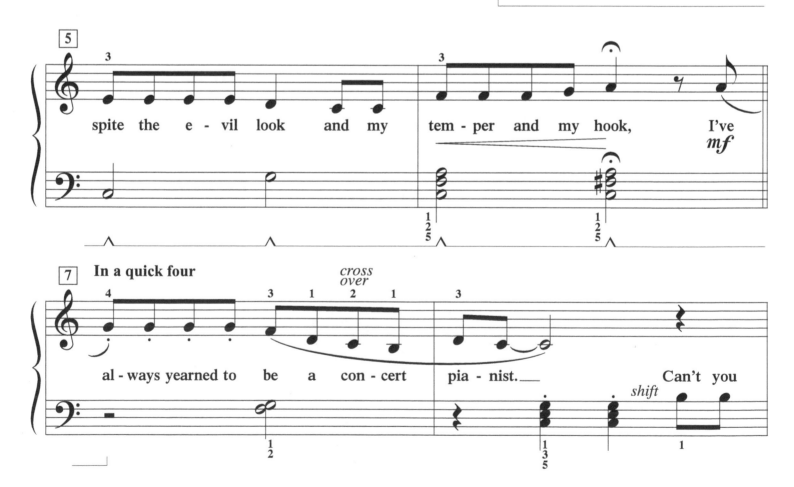

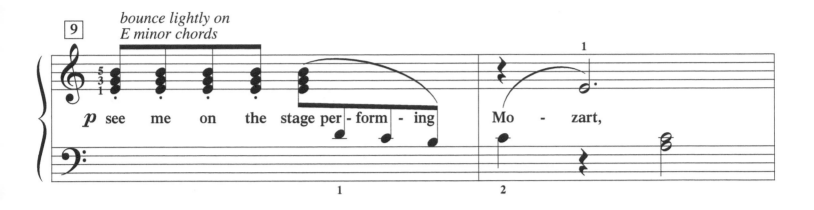

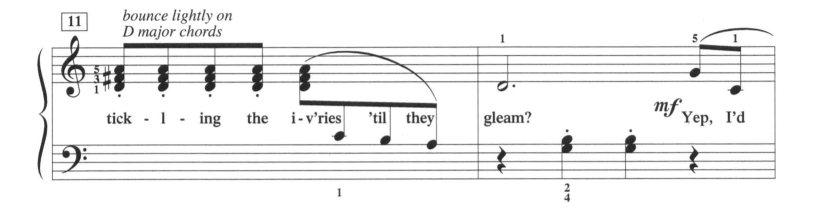

Key of G

G Scale Warm-up: Play **H.A.** (Hands Alone), then **H.T.** (Hands Together).

Chord Warm-up:

I Just Can't Wait to Be King

from *THE LION KING*

WHO SAID THIS?
My dad just showed me the whole kingdom. And I'm gonna rule it all.

Music by ELTON JOHN
Lyrics by TIM RICE

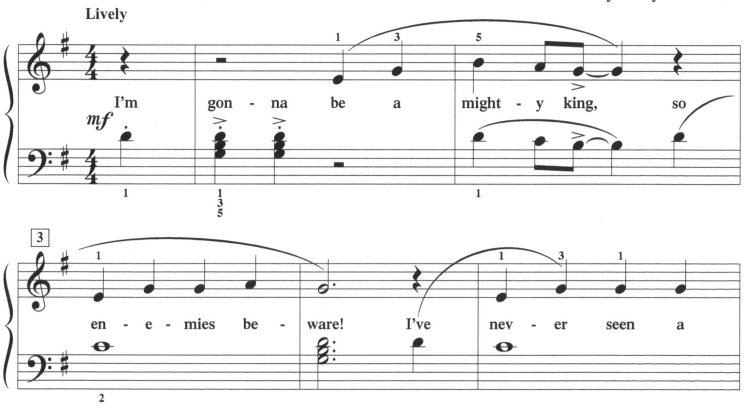

ANSWER: Simba

FF3042

14

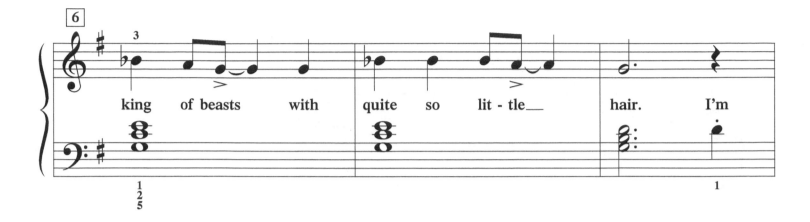

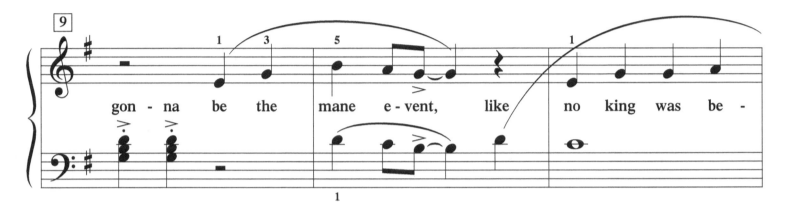

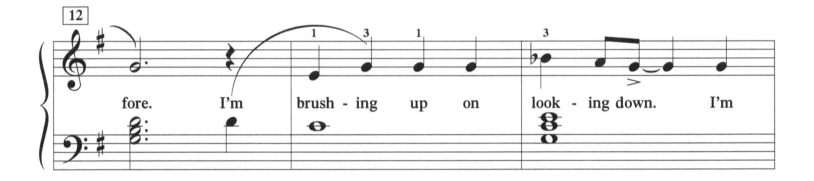

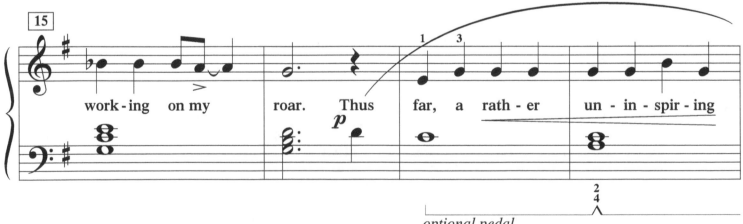

optional pedal

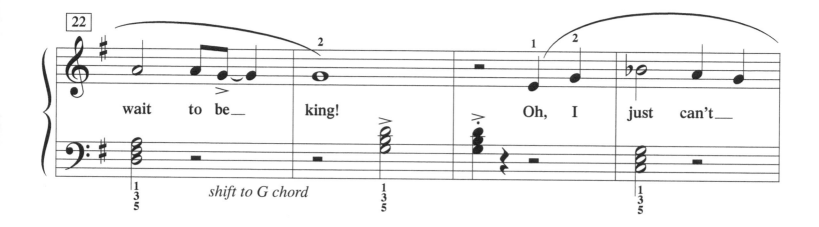

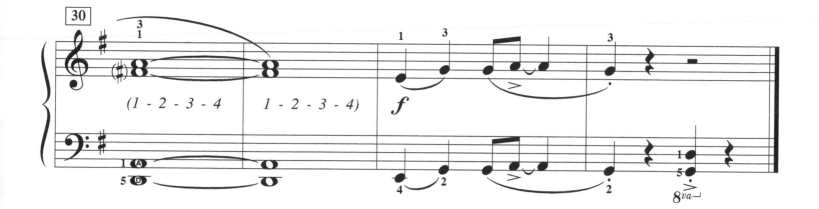

16

Bella Notte

from *Lady and the Tramp*

WHO SAID THIS?
Look, there's a great big hunk of world down there with no fence around it. Where two dogs can find adventure and excitement.

Music and Lyrics by
PEGGY LEE and
SONNY BURKE

take the love of your loved one. You'll

need it a-bout this time, *(p)* to keep from fall-ing

like a star when you make that diz-zy climb. For

this is the night and the heav-ens are right on this

love-ly bel-la not-te.

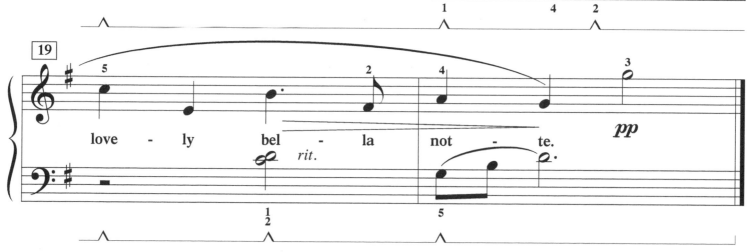

Circle of Life

from *The Lion King*

WHO SAID THIS?
Everything the light touches is our kingdom.

Music by ELTON JOHN
Lyrics by TIM RICE

Moderately

mp From the day we ar - rive on the plan - et and

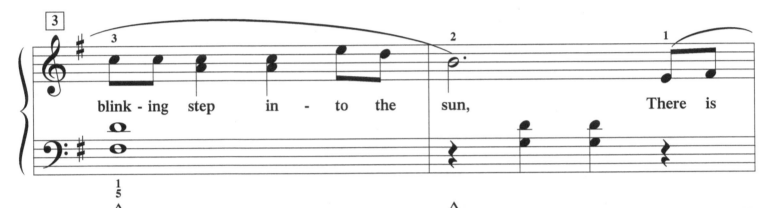

blink - ing step in - to the sun, There is

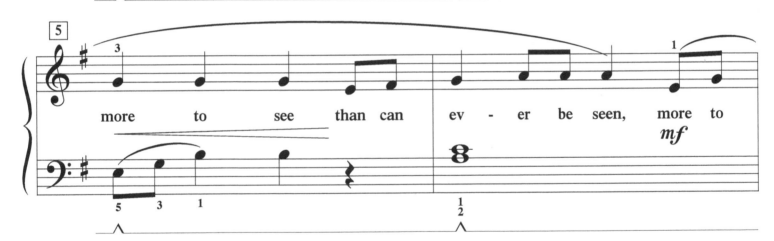

more to see than can ev - er be seen, more to *mf*

do than can ev - er be done. There is *mp*

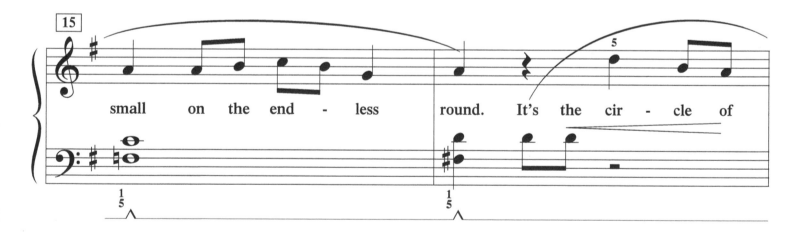

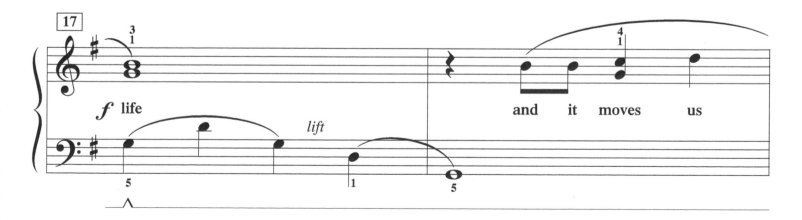

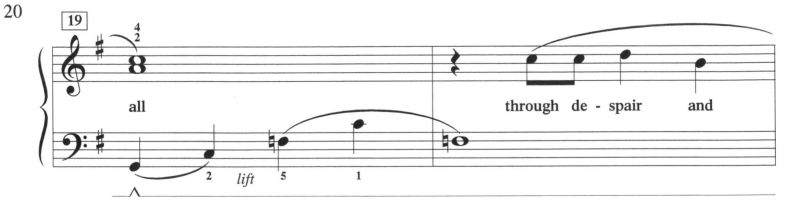

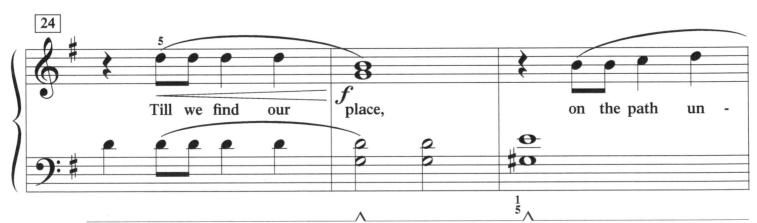

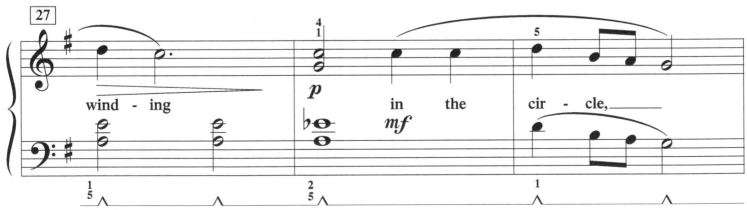

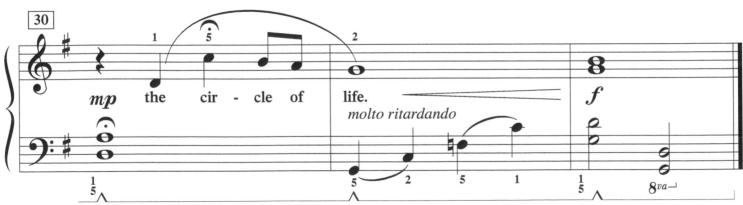

Key of F

F Scale Warm-up: Play **H.A.** (Hands Alone), then **H.T.** (Hands Together).

Chord Warm-up:

The Bare Necessities

from *The Jungle Book*

Words and Music by
TERRY GILKYSON

Bright and snappy

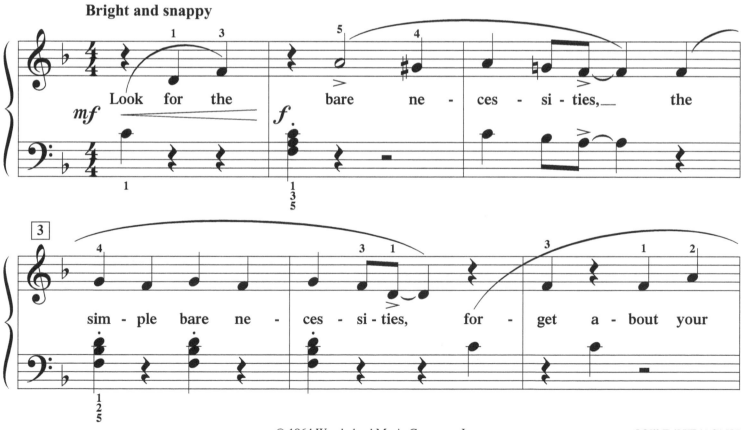

Look for the bare ne - ces - si - ties,___ the

sim - ple bare ne - ces - si - ties, for - get a - bout your

ANSWER: Baloo

FF3042

22

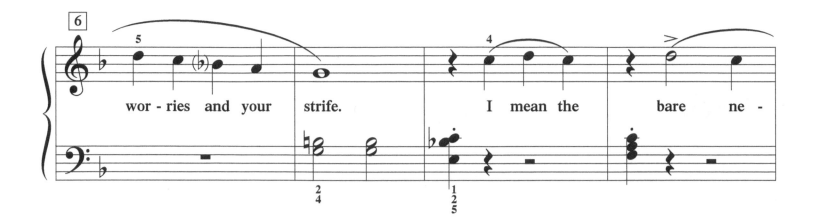

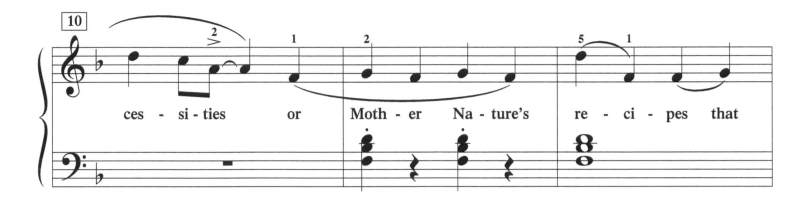

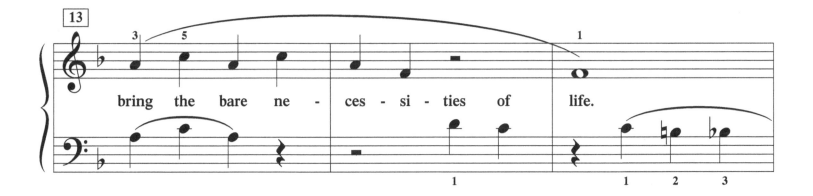

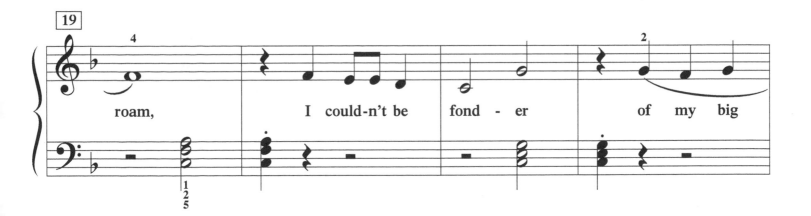

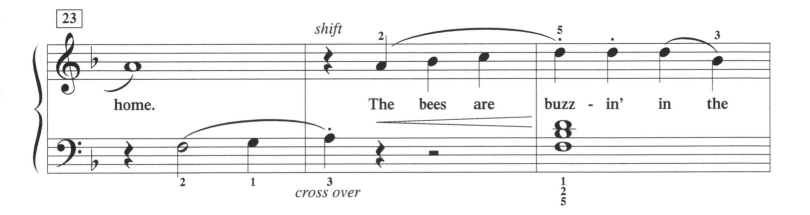

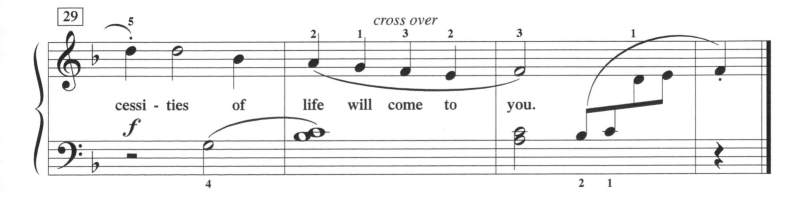

Fathoms Below

from *THE LITTLE MERMAID*

WHO SAID THIS?
Isn't this great? The salty sea air.
The wind blowing in your face.
Perfect day to be at sea!

Music by ALAN MENKEN
Lyrics by HOWARD ASHMAN

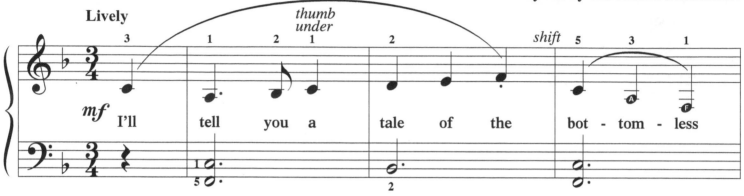

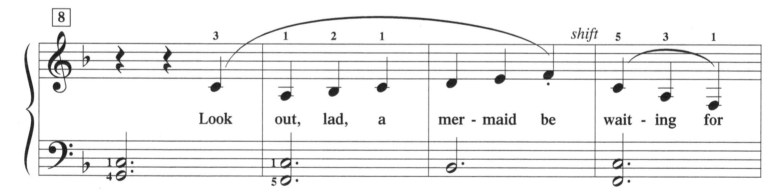

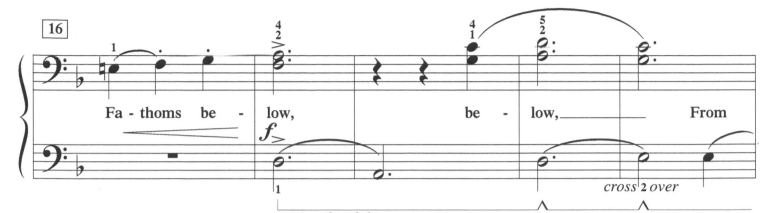

Fa - thoms be - low, be - low,_____ From

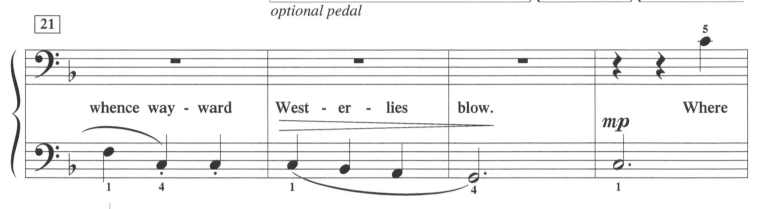

whence way - ward West - er - lies blow. Where

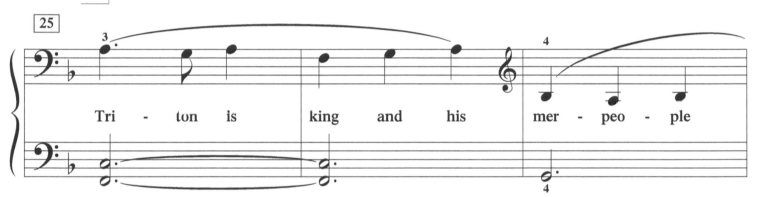

Tri - ton is king and his mer - peo - ple

sing in mys - te - ri - ous fa - thoms be - low.

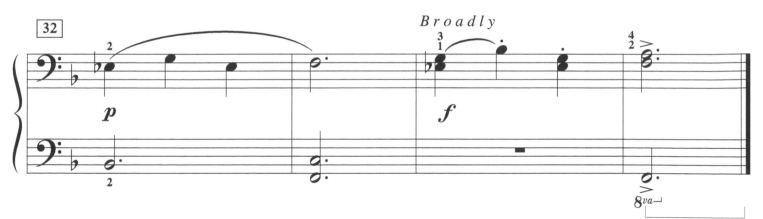

FF3042

How Far I'll Go

from *Moana*

Music and Lyrics by
LIN-MANUEL MIRANDA

Moderately fast

mp I've been star - ing at the edge of the wa - ter long___

___ as I can re - mem - ber, nev - er real - ly know-ing

why. I wish I could be the per-fect

daugh - ter but I come back to (the) wa - ter no

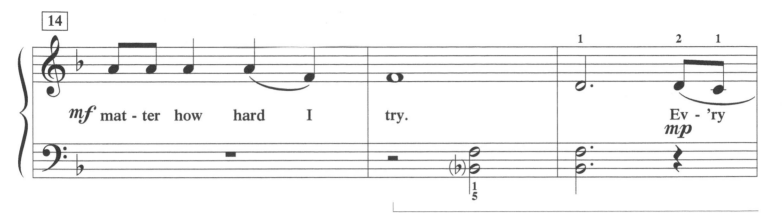

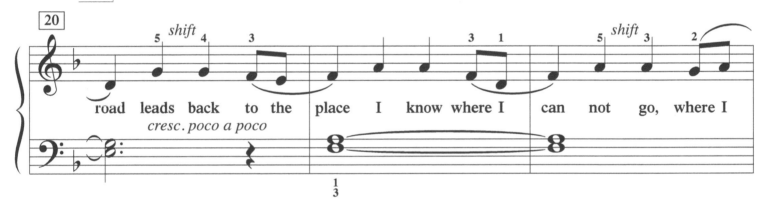

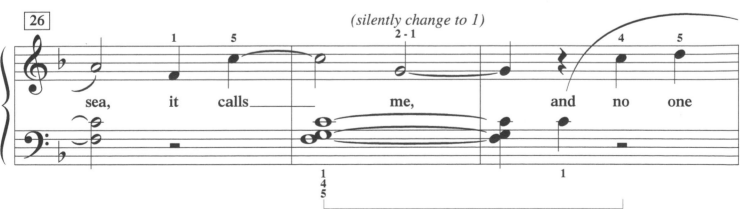

knows_____ how far it goes._____

If the wind in my sail on the sea stays be - hind_____

me, One day I'll know._____

If I go, there's just no telling how far I'll
rit.

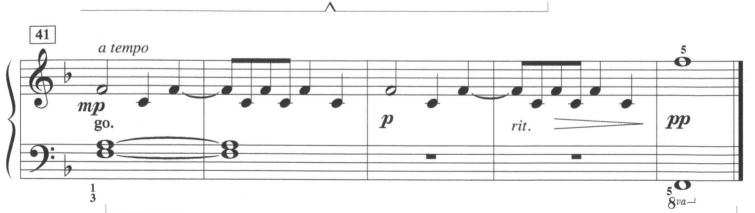

a tempo

mp
go.

p

rit.

pp

8va